This Reading Log Book
Belongs To :

_____

_____

Number	Book Title	Kind Of Your Book	Kind Of Your Book	Kind Of Your Book	Kind Of Your Book	Kind Of Your Book	Kind Of Your Book	Kind Of Your Book
1								
2								
3								
4								
5								
6								
7								
8								
9								
10								
11								
12								
13								
14								
15								
16								
17								
18								
19								
20								

Number	Book Title							
21								
22								
23								
24								
25								
26								
27								
28								
29								
30								
31								
32								
33								
34								
35								
36								
37								
38								
39								
40								

Number	Book Title	Kind Of Your Book	Kind Of Your Book	Kind Of Your Book	Kind Of Your Book	Kind Of Your Book	Kind Of Your Book	Kind Of Your Book
41								
42								
43								
44								
45								
46								
47								
48								
49								
50								
51								
52								
53								
54								
55								
56								
57								
58								
59								
60								

Number	Book Title	Kind Of Your Book	Kind Of Your Book	Kind Of Your Book	Kind Of Your Book	Kind Of Your Book	Kind Of Your Book	Kind Of Your Book
61								
62								
63								
64								
65								
56								
76								
68								
69								
70								
71								
72								
73								
74								
75								
76								
77								
78								
79								
80								

Number	Book Title	Rate of Your Book	Rate of Your Book	Rate of Your Book	Rate of Your Book	Rate of Your Book	Rate of Your Book	Rate of Your Book
81								
82								
83								
84								
85								
86								
87								
88								
89								
90								
91								
92								
93								
94								
95								
96								
97								
98								
99								
100								

Today
a reader,
Tomorrow
a leader

Margaret Fuller

Ratings

Plot : ☆ ☆ ☆ ☆ ☆

Characters : ☐ ☐ ☐ ☐ ☐

Ease of reading : ◇ ◇ ◇ ◇ ◇

Over All : ☹ 😐 🙂

○ Paperback

○ Hardbook

○ E - Book

○ Audiobook

TITLE :

Author :

Publisher : _____ Pub. Date _____ Page Count _____

○ Fiction   ○ Non - Fiction

Genre · _____ Subject : _____

Review : _____

Dates

Start :

Finished :

How I Got This Book

☐ Bought It

☐ Checked Out From Library

☐ Borrowed From

....

☐ Gift From

....

Favorite Quotes From The Book

Book Number

Ratings

Plot : ☆ ☆ ☆ ☆ ☆

Characters : ☐ ☐ ☐ ☐ ☐

Ease of reading : ◇ ◇ ◇ ◇ ◇

Over All : ☹ 😐 🙂

○ Paperback
○ Hardbook
○ E - Book
○ Audiobook

TITLE :

Anthor :

Publisher : _____ Pub. Date _____ Page Count _____

○ Fiction   ○ Non - Fiction

Genre · _____ Subject : _____

Review : _____

Dates

Start :

Finished :

How I Got This Book

☐ Bought It

☐ Checked Out From Library

☐ Borrowed From

....

☐ Gift From

....

Favorite Quotes From The Book

Ratings

Plot : ☆ ☆ ☆ ☆ ☆

Characters : ☐ ☐ ☐ ☐ ☐

Ease of reading : ◇ ◇ ◇ ◇ ◇

Over All : ☹ 😐 🙂

Book Number

○ Paperback

○ Hardbook

○ E - Book

○ Audiobook

TITLE :

Anthor :

Publisher : _____ Pub. Date _____ Page Count _____

○ Fiction   ○ Non - Fiction

Genre · _____   Subject : _____

Review : _____

Dates

Start :

Finished :

How I Got This Book

☐ Bought It

☐ Checked Out From Library

☐ Borrowed From
....

☐ Gift From
....

Favorite Quotes From The Book

Ratings

Plot : ☆ ☆ ☆ ☆ ☆

Characters : ☐ ☐ ☐ ☐ ☐

Ease of reading : ◇ ◇ ◇ ◇ ◇

Over All : ☹ 😐 🙂

○ Paperback

○ Hardbook

○ E - Book

○ Audiobook

BookNumber

TITLE :

Author :

Publisher : _____ Pub. Date _____ Page Count _____

○ Fiction ○ Non - Fiction

Genre _____ Subject : _____

Review : _____

Dates

Start :

Finished :

How I Got This Book

☐ Bought It

☐ Checked Out From Library

☐ Borrowed From

☐ Gift From

Favorite Quotes From The Book

Book Number

Ratings

Plot : ☆ ☆ ☆ ☆ ☆

Characters : ☐ ☐ ☐ ☐ ☐

Ease of reading : ◇ ◇ ◇ ◇ ◇

Over All : ☹ 😐 🙂

○ Paperback

○ Hardbook

○ E - Book

○ Audiobook

TITLE :

Author :

Publisher : _____ Pub. Date _____ Page Count _____

○ Fiction   ○ Non - Fiction

Genre · _____   Subject : _____

Review : _____

Dates

Start :

Finished :

How I Got This Book

☐ Bought It

☐ Checked Out From Library

☐ Borrowed From

....

☐ Gift From

....

Favorite Quotes From The Book

Rank Number

Ratings

Plot : ☆ ☆ ☆ ☆ ☆

Characters : ☐ ☐ ☐ ☐ ☐

Ease of reading : ◇ ◇ ◇ ◇ ◇

Over All : ☹ 😐 ☺

○ Paperback

○ Hardbook

○ E - Book

○ Audiobook

TITLE :

Anthor :

Publisher : _____ Pub. Date _____ Page Count _____

○ Fiction   ○ Non - Fiction

Genre · _____   Subject : _____

Review : _____

Dates

Start :

Finished :

How I Got This Book

☐ Bought It

☐ Checked Out From Library

☐ Borrowed From

....

☐ Gift From

....

Favorite Quotes From The Book

Ratings

Plot : ☆ ☆ ☆ ☆ ☆

Characters : ☐ ☐ ☐ ☐ ☐

Ease of reading : ◇ ◇ ◇ ◇ ◇

Over All : ☹ 😐 ☺

○ Paperback

○ Hardbook

○ E - Book

○ Audiobook

BookNumber

TITLE :

Author :

Publisher :   Pub. Date   Page Count

○ Fiction   ○ Non - Fiction

Genre ·   Subject :

Review :

Dates

Start :

Finished :

How I Got This Book

☐ Bought It

☐ Checked Out From Library

☐ Borrowed From

....

☐ Gift From

....

Favorite Quotes From The Book

Ratings

Book Number

Plot : ☆ ☆ ☆ ☆ ☆

Characters : ☐ ☐ ☐ ☐ ☐

Ease of reading : ◇ ◇ ◇ ◇ ◇

Over All : ☹ 😐 🙂

○ Paperback

○ Hardbook

○ E - Book

○ Audiobook

TITLE :

Anthor :

Publisher : _____ Pub. Date _____ Page Count _____

○ Fiction   ○ Non - Fiction

Genre · _____ Subject : _____

Review : _____

Dates

Start :

Finished :

How I Got This Book

☐ Bought It

☐ Checked Out From Library

☐ Borrowed From
....

☐ Gift From
....

Favorite Quotes From The Book

Book Number

Ratings

Plot : ☆ ☆ ☆ ☆ ☆

Characters : ☐ ☐ ☐ ☐ ☐

Ease of reading : ◇ ◇ ◇ ◇ ◇

Over All : ☹ 😐 ☺

○ Paperback

○ Hardbook

○ E - Book

○ Audiobook

TITLE :

Author :

Publisher : _____ Pub. Date _____ Page Count _____

○ Fiction   ○ Non - Fiction

Genre · _____   Subject : _____

Review : _____

Dates

Start :

Finished :

How I Got This Book

☐ Bought It

☐ Checked Out From Library

☐ Borrowed From

....

☐ Gift From

....

Favorite Quotes From The Book

Ratings

Plot : ☆ ☆ ☆ ☆ ☆

Characters : ☐ ☐ ☐ ☐ ☐

Ease of reading : ◇ ◇ ◇ ◇ ◇

Over All : ☹ 😐 🙂

Book Number

○ Paperback

○ Hardbook

○ E - Book

○ Audiobook

TITLE :

Author :

Publisher : _____ Pub. Date _____ Page Count _____

○ Fiction   ○ Non - Fiction

Genre : _____   Subject : _____

Review : _____

Dates

Start :

Finished :

How I Got This Book

☐ Bought It

☐ Checked Out From Library

☐ Borrowed From

....

☐ Gift From

....

Favorite Quotes From The Book

Ratings

Book Number

Plot : ☆ ☆ ☆ ☆ ☆

Characters : ☐ ☐ ☐ ☐ ☐

Ease of reading : ◇ ◇ ◇ ◇ ◇

Over All : ☹ 😐 😊

○ Paperback

○ Hardbook

○ E - Book

○ Audiobook

TITLE :

Anthor :

Publisher : _____ Pub. Date _____ Page Count _____

○ Fiction   ○ Non - Fiction

Genre · _____ Subject : _____

Review : _____

Dates

Start :

Finished :

How I Got This Book

☐ Bought It

☐ Checked Out From Library

☐ Borrowed From

....

☐ Gift From

....

Favorite Quotes From The Book

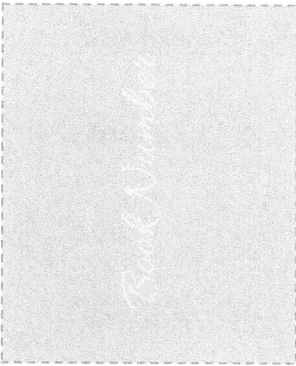

Book Number

Ratings

Plot : ☆ ☆ ☆ ☆ ☆

Characters : ☐ ☐ ☐ ☐ ☐

Ease of reading : ◇ ◇ ◇ ◇ ◇

Over All : ☹ 😐 ☺

○ Paperback

○ Hardbook

○ E - Book

○ Audiobook

TITLE :

Author :

Publisher : .... Pub. Date .... Page Count ....

○ Fiction   ○ Non - Fiction

Genre : ....   Subject : ....

Review : ....

Dates

Start :

Finished :

How I Got This Book

☐ Bought It

☐ Checked Out From Library

☐ Borrowed From

....

☐ Gift From

....

Favorite Quotes From The Book

Ratings

Plot : ☆ ☆ ☆ ☆ ☆

Characters : ☐ ☐ ☐ ☐ ☐

Ease of reading : ◇ ◇ ◇ ◇ ◇

Over All : ☹ 😐 🙂

Book Number

○ Paperback

○ Hardbook

○ E - Book

○ Audiobook

TITLE :

Author :

Publisher : _____ Pub. Date _____ Page Count _____

○ Fiction   ○ Non - Fiction

Genre · _____   Subject : _____

Review : _____

Dates

Start :

Finished :

How I Got This Book

☐ Bought It

☐ Checked Out From Library

☐ Borrowed From

....

☐ Gift From

....

Favorite Quotes From The Book

Ratings

Plot : ☆ ☆ ☆ ☆ ☆

Characters : ☐ ☐ ☐ ☐ ☐

Ease of reading : ◇ ◇ ◇ ◇ ◇

Over All : ☹ 😐 ☺

○ Paperback

○ Hardbook

○ E - Book

○ Audiobook

TITLE :

Author :

Publisher : _____ Pub. Date _____ Page Count _____

○ Fiction   ○ Non - Fiction

Genre : _____   Subject : _____

Review :

Dates

Start :

Finished :

How I Got This Book

☐ Bought It

☐ Checked Out From Library

☐ Borrowed From
....

☐ Gift From
....

Favorite Quotes From The Book

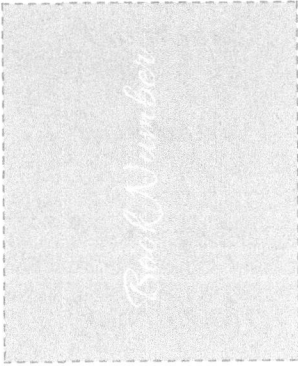

Ratings

Plot : ☆ ☆ ☆ ☆ ☆

Characters : ☐ ☐ ☐ ☐ ☐

Ease of reading : ◇ ◇ ◇ ◇ ◇

Over All : ☹ 😐 🙂

○ Paperback

○ Hardbook

○ E - Book

○ Audiobook

TITLE :

Author :

Publisher : _____ Pub. Date _____ Page Count _____

○ Fiction   ○ Non - Fiction

Genre : _____ Subject : _____

Review : _____

Dates

Start :

Finished :

How I Got This Book

☐ Bought It

☐ Checked Out From Library

☐ Borrowed From

....

☐ Gift From

....

Favorite Quotes From The Book

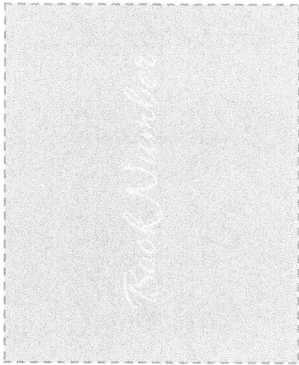

Ratings

Plot : ☆ ☆ ☆ ☆ ☆

Characters : ▢ ▢ ▢ ▢ ▢

Ease of reading : ◇ ◇ ◇ ◇ ◇

Over All : ☹ 😐 🙂

○ Paperback
○ Hardbook
○ E - Book
○ Audiobook

TITLE :

Anthor :

Publisher : _____ Pub. Date _____ Page Count _____

○ Fiction   ○ Non - Fiction

Genre : _____ Subject : _____

Review : _____

Dates

Start :

Finished :

How I Got This Book

☐ Bought It

☐ Checked Out From Library

☐ Borrowed From
....

☐ Gift From
....

Favorite Quotes From The Book

BookNumber

Ratings

Plot : ☆ ☆ ☆ ☆ ☆

Characters : ☐ ☐ ☐ ☐ ☐

Ease of reading : ◇ ◇ ◇ ◇ ◇

Over All : 😞 😐 🙂

○ Paperback

○ Hardbook

○ E - Book

○ Audiobook

TITLE :

Anthor :

Publisher : .... Pub. Date .... Page Count ....

○ Fiction   ○ Non - Fiction

Genre · ....   Subject : ....

Review : ....

Dates

Start :

Finished :

How I Got This Book

☐ Bought It

☐ Checked Out From Library

☐ Borrowed From

....

☐ Gift From

....

Favorite Qyotes From The Book

Ratings

Plot : ☆ ☆ ☆ ☆ ☆

Characters : ☐ ☐ ☐ ☐ ☐

Ease of reading : ◇ ◇ ◇ ◇ ◇

Over All : ☹ 😐 🙂

○ Paperback

○ Hardbook

○ E - Book

○ Audiobook

Book Number

TITLE :

Anthor :

Publisher : ____ Pub. Date ____ Page Count ____

○ Fiction   ○ Non - Fiction

Genre : ____   Subject : ____

Review : ____

Dates

Start :

Finished :

How I Got This Book

☐ Bought It

☐ Checked Out From Library

☐ Borrowed From

....

☐ Gift From

....

Favorite Quotes From The Book

Ratings

Plot : ☆ ☆ ☆ ☆ ☆

Characters : ☐ ☐ ☐ ☐ ☐

Ease of reading : ◇ ◇ ◇ ◇ ◇

Over All : ☹ 😐 🙂

○ Paperback

○ Hardbook

○ E - Book

○ Audiobook

TITLE :

Author :

Publisher : .... Pub. Date .... Page Count ....

○ Fiction ○ Non - Fiction

Genre .... Subject : ....

Review : ....

Dates

Start :

Finished :

How I Got This Book

☐ Bought It

☐ Checked Out From Library

☐ Borrowed From
....

☐ Gift From
....

Favorite Quotes From The Book

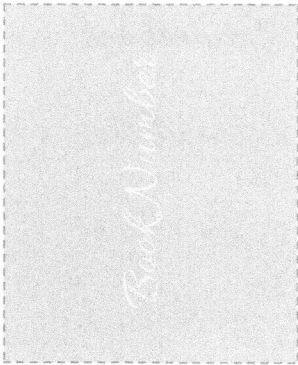

Ratings

Plot : ☆ ☆ ☆ ☆ ☆

Characters : ☐ ☐ ☐ ☐ ☐

Ease of reading : ◇ ◇ ◇ ◇ ◇

Over All : ☹ 😐 ☺

○ Paperback

○ Hardbook

○ E - Book

○ Audiobook

TITLE :

Author :

Publisher : _____ Pub. Date _____ Page Count _____

○ Fiction   ○ Non - Fiction

Genre · _____ Subject : _____

Review : _____

Dates

Start :

Finished :

How I Got This Book

☐ Bought It

☐ Checked Out From Library

☐ Borrowed From

....

☐ Gift From

....

Favorite Quotes From The Book

Ratings

Plot : ☆ ☆ ☆ ☆ ☆

Characters : ☐ ☐ ☐ ☐ ☐

Ease of reading : ◇ ◇ ◇ ◇ ◇

Over All : ☹ 😐 🙂

○ Paperback

○ Hardbook

○ E - Book

○ Audiobook

Book Number

TITLE :

Author :

Publisher : _____ Pub. Date _____ Page Count _____

○ Fiction   ○ Non - Fiction

Genre · _____   Subject : _____

Review : _____

Dates

Start :

Finished :

How I Got This Book

☐ Bought It

☐ Checked Out From Library

☐ Borrowed From

....

☐ Gift From

....

Favorite Quotes From The Book

Book Number

Ratings

Plot : ☆ ☆ ☆ ☆ ☆

Characters : ☐ ☐ ☐ ☐ ☐

Ease of reading : ◇ ◇ ◇ ◇ ◇

Over All : ☹ 😐 🙂

○ Paperback

○ Hardbook

○ E - Book

○ Audiobook

TITLE :

Author :

Publisher : .... Pub. Date .... Page Count ....

○ Fiction   ○ Non - Fiction

Genre : ....   Subject : ....

Review : ....

Dates

Start :

Finished :

How I Got This Book

☐ Bought It

☐ Checked Out From Library

☐ Borrowed From

....

☐ Gift From

....

Favorite Quotes From The Book

Ratings

Plot : ☆ ☆ ☆ ☆ ☆

Characters : ☐ ☐ ☐ ☐ ☐

Ease of reading : ◇ ◇ ◇ ◇ ◇

Over All : ☹ 😐 🙂

○ Paperback

○ Hardbook

○ E - Book

○ Audiobook

Book Number

TITLE :

Anthor :

Publisher : _____ Pub. Date _____ Page Count _____

○ Fiction   ○ Non - Fiction

Genre · _____ Subject : _____

Review : _____

Dates

Start :

Finished :

How I Got This Book

☐ Bought It

☐ Checked Out From Library

☐ Borrowed From
....

☐ Gift From
....

Favorite Quotes From The Book

Book Number

Ratings

Plot : ☆ ☆ ☆ ☆ ☆

Characters : ☐ ☐ ☐ ☐ ☐

Ease of reading : ◇ ◇ ◇ ◇ ◇

Over All : ☹ ☺ ☺

○ Paperback

○ Hardbook

○ E - Book

○ Audiobook

TITLE :

Author :

Publisher : _____ Pub. Date _____ Page Count _____

○ Fiction   ○ Non - Fiction

Genre · _____ Subject : _____

Review : _____

Dates

Start :

Finished :

How I Got This Book

☐ Bought It

☐ Checked Out From Library

☐ Borrowed From

....

☐ Gift From

....

Favorite Quotes From The Book

Ratings

Plot : ☆ ☆ ☆ ☆ ☆

Characters : ☐ ☐ ☐ ☐ ☐

Ease of reading : ◇ ◇ ◇ ◇ ◇

Over All : ☹ 😐 🙂

○ Paperback

○ Hardbook

○ E - Book

○ Audiobook

Book Number

TITLE :

Author :

Publisher : _____ Pub. Date _____ Page Count _____

○ Fiction   ○ Non - Fiction

Genre · _____ Subject : _____

Review : _____

Dates

Start :

Finished :

How I Got This Book

☐ Bought It

☐ Checked Out From Library

☐ Borrowed From
....

☐ Gift From
....

Favorite Quotes From The Book

Rank Number

Ratings

Plot : ☆ ☆ ☆ ☆ ☆

Characters : ☐ ☐ ☐ ☐ ☐

Ease of reading : ◇ ◇ ◇ ◇ ◇

Over All : ☹ 😐 ☺

○ Paperback

○ Hardbook

○ E - Book

○ Audiobook

TITLE :

Anthor :

Publisher : _____ Pub. Date _____ Page Count _____

○ Fiction   ○ Non - Fiction

Genre · _____   Subject : _____

Review : _____

Dates

Start :

Finished :

How I Got This Book

☐ Bought It

☐ Checked Out From Library

☐ Borrowed From

_____

☐ Gift From

_____

Favorite Quotes From The Book

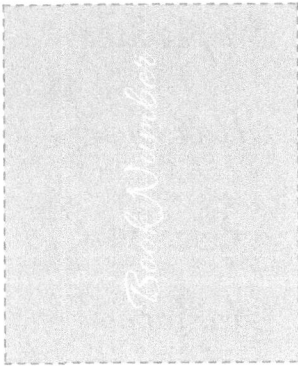

Book Number

Ratings

Plot : ☆ ☆ ☆ ☆ ☆

Characters : ☐ ☐ ☐ ☐ ☐

Ease of reading : ◇ ◇ ◇ ◇ ◇

Over All : ☹ 😐 ☺

○ Paperback

○ Hardbook

○ E - Book

○ Audiobook

TITLE :

Author :

Publisher : _____ Pub. Date _____ Page Count _____

○ Fiction   ○ Non - Fiction

Genre : _____   Subject : _____

Review : _____

Dates

Start :

Finished :

How I Got This Book

☐ Bought It

☐ Checked Out From Library

☐ Borrowed From

....

☐ Gift From

....

Favorite Quotes From The Book

Ratings

Plot : ☆ ☆ ☆ ☆ ☆

Characters : ☐ ☐ ☐ ☐ ☐

Ease of reading : ◇ ◇ ◇ ◇ ◇

Over All : ︵ ⊡ ☺

○ Paperback

○ Hardbook

○ E - Book

○ Audiobook

TITLE :

Anthor :

Publisher : _____ Pub. Date _____ Page Count _____

○ Fiction   ○ Non - Fiction

Genre : _____   Subject : _____

Review : _____

Dates

Start :

Finished :

How I Got This Book

☐ Bought It

☐ Checked Out From Library

☐ Borrowed From

....

☐ Gift From

....

Favorite Quotes From The Book

Book Number

Ratings

Plot : ☆ ☆ ☆ ☆ ☆

Characters : ☐ ☐ ☐ ☐ ☐

Ease of reading : ◇ ◇ ◇ ◇ ◇

Over All : ☹ 😐 ☺

○ Paperback

○ Hardbook

○ E - Book

○ Audiobook

TITLE :

Author :

Publisher : _____ Pub. Date _____ Page Count _____

○ Fiction   ○ Non - Fiction

Genre · _____   Subject : _____

Review : _____

Dates

Start :

Finished :

How I Got This Book

☐ Bought It

☐ Checked Out From Library

☐ Borrowed From

....

☐ Gift From

....

Favorite Quotes From The Book

Book Number

Ratings

Plot : ☆ ☆ ☆ ☆ ☆

Characters : ☐ ☐ ☐ ☐ ☐

Ease of reading : ◇ ◇ ◇ ◇ ◇

Over All : ☹ 😐 ☺

○ Paperback

○ Hardbook

○ E - Book

○ Audiobook

TITLE :

Anthor :

Publisher : _____ Pub. Date _____ Page Count _____

○ Fiction   ○ Non - Fiction

Genre · _____   Subject : _____

Review :

Dates

Start :

Finished :

How I Got This Book

☐ Bought It

☐ Checked Out From Library

☐ Borrowed From

....

☐ Gift From

....

Favorite Quotes From The Book

Book Number

Ratings

Plot : ☆ ☆ ☆ ☆ ☆

Characters : ☐ ☐ ☐ ☐ ☐

Ease of reading : ◇ ◇ ◇ ◇ ◇

Over All : ☹ 😐 🙂

○ Paperback

○ Hardbook

○ E - Book

○ Audiobook

TITLE :

Author :

Publisher : _____ Pub. Date _____ Page Count _____

○ Fiction   ○ Non - Fiction

Genre · _____   Subject : _____

Review : _____

Dates

Start :

Finished :

How I Got This Book

☐ Bought It

☐ Checked Out From Library

☐ Borrowed From

....

☐ Gift From

....

Favorite Quotes From The Book

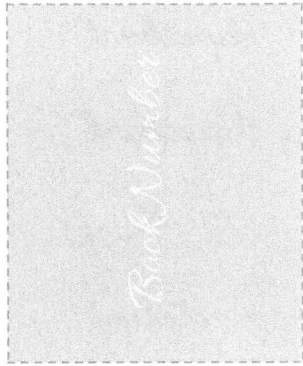

Book Number

Ratings

Plot : ☆ ☆ ☆ ☆ ☆

Characters : ☐ ☐ ☐ ☐ ☐

Ease of reading : ◇ ◇ ◇ ◇ ◇

Over All : ☹ 😐 ☺

○ Paperback

○ Hardbook

○ E - Book

○ Audiobook

TITLE :

Anthor :

Publisher : _____ Pub. Date _____ Page Count _____

○ Fiction   ○ Non - Fiction

Genre · _____   Subject : _____

Review : _____

Dates

Start :

Finished :

How I Got This Book

☐ Bought It

☐ Checked Out From Library

☐ Borrowed From
....

☐ Gift From
....

Favorite Quotes From The Book

Book Number

Ratings

Plot : ☆ ☆ ☆ ☆ ☆

Characters : ☐ ☐ ☐ ☐ ☐

Ease of reading : ◇ ◇ ◇ ◇ ◇

Over All : ☹ ☺ ☺

○ Paperback

○ Hardbook

○ E - Book

○ Audiobook

TITLE :

Author :

Publisher : _____ Pub. Date _____ Page Count _____

○ Fiction   ○ Non - Fiction

Genre · _____ Subject : _____

Review : _____

Dates

Start :

Finished :

How I Got This Book

☐ Bought It

☐ Checked Out From Library

☐ Borrowed From

....

☐ Gift From

....

Favorite Quotes From The Book

Book Number

Ratings

Plot : ☆ ☆ ☆ ☆ ☆

Characters : ☐ ☐ ☐ ☐ ☐

Ease of reading : ◇ ◇ ◇ ◇ ◇

Over All : ☹ 😐 🙂

○ Paperback

○ Hardbook

○ E - Book

○ Audiobook

TITLE :

Anthor :

Publisher :   Pub. Date   Page Count

○ Fiction   ○ Non - Fiction

Genre ·   Subject :

Review :

Dates

Start :

Finished :

How I Got This Book

☐ Bought It

☐ Checked Out From Library

☐ Borrowed From

....

☐ Gift From

....

Favorite Quotes From The Book

Ratings

Plot : ☆ ☆ ☆ ☆ ☆

Characters : ☐ ☐ ☐ ☐ ☐

Ease of reading : ◇ ◇ ◇ ◇ ◇

Over All : ︵ ︵   ⋯   ‿

○ Paperback

○ Hardbook

○ E - Book

○ Audiobook

TITLE :

Anthor :

Publisher :　　　　　　Pub. Date　　　　　　Page Count

○ Fiction　　　　　　○ Non - Fiction

Genre ·　　　　　　Subject :

Review :

Dates

Start :

Finished :

How I Got This Book

☐ Bought It

☐ Checked Out From Library

☐ Borrowed From

....

☐ Gift From

....

Favorite Quotes From The Book

Book Number

Ratings

Plot : ☆ ☆ ☆ ☆ ☆

Characters : ☐ ☐ ☐ ☐ ☐

Ease of reading : ◇ ◇ ◇ ◇ ◇

Over All : ☹ 😐 🙂

○ Paperback

○ Hardbook

○ E - Book

○ Audiobook

TITLE :

Anthor :

Publisher : _____   Pub. Date _____   Page Count _____

Dates

○ Fiction   ○ Non - Fiction

Genre · _____   Subject : _____

Start :

Finished :

Review : _____

How I Got This Book

☐ Bought It

☐ Checked Out From Library

☐ Borrowed From

....

☐ Gift From

....

Favorite Quotes From The Book

Ratings

Plot : ☆ ☆ ☆ ☆ ☆

Characters : ☐ ☐ ☐ ☐ ☐

Ease of reading : ◇ ◇ ◇ ◇ ◇

Over All : ☹ 😐 ☺

○ Paperback

○ Hardbook

○ E - Book

○ Audiobook

Book Number

TITLE :

Anthor :

Publisher : _____ Pub. Date _____ Page Count _____

○ Fiction   ○ Non - Fiction

Genre · _____   Subject : _____

Review : _____

Dates

Start :

Finished :

How I Got This Book

☐ Bought It

☐ Checked Out From Library

☐ Borrowed From

....

☐ Gift From

....

Favorite Quotes From The Book

Ratings

Plot : ☆ ☆ ☆ ☆ ☆

Characters : ☐ ☐ ☐ ☐ ☐

Ease of reading : ◇ ◇ ◇ ◇ ◇

Over All : ☹ 😐 🙂

○ Paperback

○ Hardbook

○ E - Book

○ Audiobook

Book Number

TITLE :

Anthor :

Publisher : _____ Pub. Date _____ Page Count _____

○ Fiction   ○ Non - Fiction

Genre · _____   Subject : _____

Review : _____

Dates

Start :

Finished :

How I Got This Book

☐ Bought It

☐ Checked Out From Library

☐ Borrowed From

....

☐ Gift From

....

Favorite Quotes From The Book

Ratings

Plot : ☆ ☆ ☆ ☆ ☆

Characters : ☐ ☐ ☐ ☐ ☐

Ease of reading : ◇ ◇ ◇ ◇ ◇

Over All : ☹ 😐 🙂

○ Paperback

○ Hardbook

○ E - Book

○ Audiobook

TITLE :

Author :

Publisher : _____ Pub. Date _____ Page Count _____

○ Fiction   ○ Non - Fiction

Genre · _____ Subject : _____

Review : _____

Dates

Start :

Finished :

How I Got This Book

☐ Bought It

☐ Checked Out From Library

☐ Borrowed From

....

☐ Gift From

....

Favorite Quotes From The Book

Ratings

Plot : ☆ ☆ ☆ ☆ ☆

Characters : ☐ ☐ ☐ ☐ ☐

Ease of reading : ◇ ◇ ◇ ◇ ◇

Over All : ☹ 😐 😊

○ Paperback

○ Hardbook

○ E - Book

○ Audiobook

Book Number

TITLE :

Anthor :

Publisher : _____ Pub. Date _____ Page Count _____

○ Fiction   ○ Non - Fiction

Genre · _____   Subject : _____

Review : _____

Dates

Start :

Finished :

How I Got This Book

☐ Bought It

☐ Checked Out From Library

☐ Borrowed From

....

☐ Gift From

....

Favorite Quotes From The Book

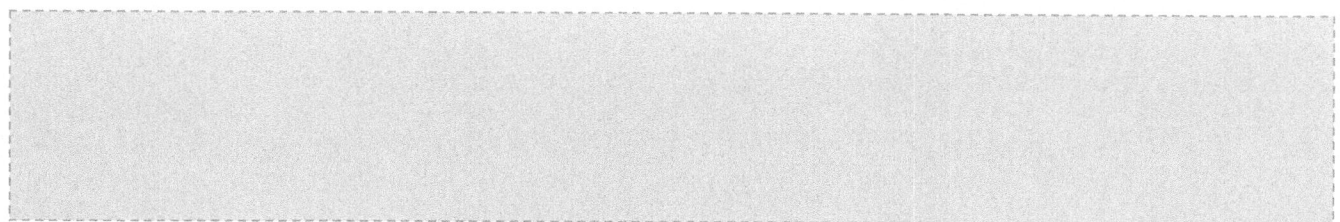

Ratings

Plot : ☆ ☆ ☆ ☆ ☆

Characters : ☐ ☐ ☐ ☐ ☐

Ease of reading : ◇ ◇ ◇ ◇ ◇

Over All : ☹ 😐 😊

○ Paperback

○ Hardbook

○ E - Book

○ Audiobook

Book Number

TITLE :

Anthor :

Publisher : _____ Pub. Date _____ Page Count _____

○ Fiction   ○ Non - Fiction

Genre · _____   Subject : _____

Review : _____

Dates

Start :

Finished :

How I Got This Book

☐ Bought It

☐ Checked Out From Library

☐ Borrowed From
....

☐ Gift From
....

Favorite Quotes From The Book

Ratings

Plot : ☆ ☆ ☆ ☆ ☆

Characters : ☐ ☐ ☐ ☐ ☐

Ease of reading : ◇ ◇ ◇ ◇ ◇

Over All : ☹ 😐 😊

○ Paperback

○ Hardbook

○ E - Book

○ Audiobook

TITLE :

Anthor :

Publisher : _____ Pub. Date _____ Page Count _____

○ Fiction ○ Non - Fiction

Genre · _____ Subject : _____

Review : _____

Dates

Start :

Finished :

How I Got This Book

☐ Bought It

☐ Checked Out From Library

☐ Borrowed From

....

☐ Gift From

....

Favorite Quotes From The Book

Book Number

Ratings

Plot : ☆ ☆ ☆ ☆ ☆

Characters : ☐ ☐ ☐ ☐ ☐

Ease of reading : ◇ ◇ ◇ ◇ ◇

Over All : ☹ 😐 🙂

○ Paperback

○ Hardbook

○ E - Book

○ Audiobook

TITLE :

Author :

Publisher :   Pub. Date   Page Count

○ Fiction   ○ Non - Fiction

Genre ·   Subject :

Review :

Dates

Start :

Finished :

How I Got This Book

☐ Bought It

☐ Checked Out From Library

☐ Borrowed From

....

☐ Gift From

....

Favorite Quotes From The Book

Book Number

Ratings

Plot : ☆ ☆ ☆ ☆ ☆

Characters : ☐ ☐ ☐ ☐ ☐

Ease of reading : ◇ ◇ ◇ ◇ ◇

Over All : ☹ 😐 🙂

○ Paperback

○ Hardbook

○ E - Book

○ Audiobook

TITLE :

Anthor :

Publisher : _____ Pub. Date _____ Page Count _____

○ Fiction   ○ Non - Fiction

Genre · _____   Subject : _____

Review : _____

Dates

Start :

Finished :

How I Got This Book

☐ Bought It

☐ Checked Out From Library

☐ Borrowed From

....

☐ Gift From

....

Favorite Quotes From The Book

Book Number

Ratings

Plot : ☆ ☆ ☆ ☆ ☆

Characters : ☐ ☐ ☐ ☐ ☐

Ease of reading : ◇ ◇ ◇ ◇ ◇

Over All : ︵ ⸛ ☺

○ Paperback

○ Hardbook

○ E - Book

○ Audiobook

TITLE :

Author :

Publisher :   Pub. Date   Page Count

○ Fiction   ○ Non - Fiction

Genre ·   Subject :

Review :

Dates

Start :

Finished :

How I Got This Book

☐ Bought It

☐ Checked Out From Library

☐ Borrowed From

....

☐ Gift From

....

Favorite Quotes From The Book

Book Number

Ratings

Plot : ☆ ☆ ☆ ☆ ☆

Characters : ☐ ☐ ☐ ☐ ☐

Ease of reading : ◇ ◇ ◇ ◇ ◇

Over All : ☹ 😐 🙂

○ Paperback

○ Hardbook

○ E - Book

○ Audiobook

TITLE :

Author :

Publisher : _____ Pub. Date _____ Page Count _____

○ Fiction   ○ Non - Fiction

Genre : _____ Subject : _____

Review : _____

Dates

Start :

Finished :

How I Got This Book

☐ Bought It

☐ Checked Out From Library

☐ Borrowed From

....

☐ Gift From

....

Favorite Quotes From The Book

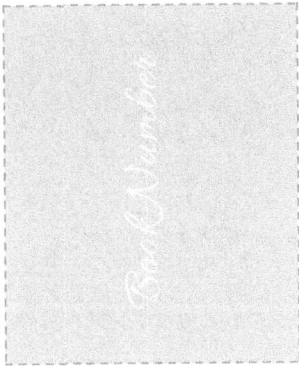

Book Number

Ratings

Plot : ☆ ☆ ☆ ☆ ☆

Characters : ☐ ☐ ☐ ☐ ☐

Ease of reading : ◇ ◇ ◇ ◇ ◇

Over All : ☹ 😐 ☺

○ Paperback

○ Hardbook

○ E - Book

○ Audiobook

TITLE :

Anthor :

Publisher : _____ Pub. Date _____ Page Count _____

○ Fiction   ○ Non - Fiction

Genre : _____ Subject : _____

Review : _____

Dates

Start :

Finished :

How I Got This Book

☐ Bought It

☐ Checked Out From Library

☐ Borrowed From

....

☐ Gift From

....

Favorite Quotes From The Book

Ratings

Plot : ☆ ☆ ☆ ☆ ☆

Characters : ☐ ☐ ☐ ☐ ☐

Ease of reading : ◇ ◇ ◇ ◇ ◇

Over All : ☹ 😐 🙂

Book Number

○ Paperback

○ Hardbook

○ E - Book

○ Audiobook

TITLE :

Author :

Publisher : _____ Pub. Date _____ Page Count _____

○ Fiction   ○ Non - Fiction

Genre : _____   Subject : _____

Review : _____

Dates

Start :

Finished :

How I Got This Book

☐ Bought It

☐ Checked Out From Library

☐ Borrowed From

....

☐ Gift From

....

Favorite Quotes From The Book

Book Number

Ratings

Plot : ☆ ☆ ☆ ☆ ☆

Characters : □ □ □ □ □

Ease of reading : ◇ ◇ ◇ ◇ ◇

Over All : ☹ 😐 🙂

○ Paperback

○ Hardbook

○ E - Book

○ Audiobook

TITLE : _____

Anthor : _____

Publisher : _____ Pub. Date _____ Page Count _____

○ Fiction   ○ Non - Fiction

Genre · _____ Subject : _____

Review : _____

Dates

Start : _____

Finished : _____

How I Got This Book

☐ Bought It

☐ Checked Out From Library

☐ Borrowed From

....

☐ Gift From

....

Favorite Qyotes From The Book

Book Number

Ratings

Plot : ☆ ☆ ☆ ☆ ☆

Characters : ☐ ☐ ☐ ☐ ☐

Ease of reading : ◇ ◇ ◇ ◇ ◇

Over All : ☹ 😐 ☺

○ Paperback

○ Hardbook

○ E - Book

○ Audiobook

TITLE :

Author :

Publisher : _____ Pub. Date _____ Page Count _____

○ Fiction   ○ Non - Fiction

Genre : _____   Subject : _____

Review : _____

Dates

Start :

Finished :

How I Got This Book

☐ Bought It

☐ Checked Out From Library

☐ Borrowed From
....

☐ Gift From
....

Favorite Quotes From The Book

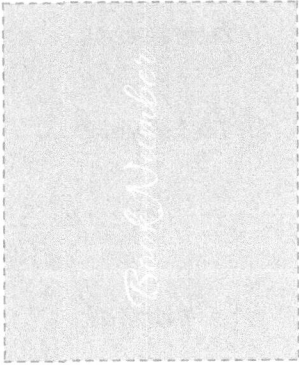

Book Number

Ratings

Plot : ☆ ☆ ☆ ☆ ☆

Characters : ☐ ☐ ☐ ☐ ☐

Ease of reading : ◇ ◇ ◇ ◇ ◇

Over All : ☹ 😐 ☺

○ Paperback

○ Hardbook

○ E - Book

○ Audiobook

TITLE : _____

Author : _____

Publisher : _____ Pub. Date _____ Page Count _____

○ Fiction   ○ Non - Fiction

Genre · _____ Subject : _____

Review : _____
_____
_____
_____
_____
_____
_____
_____

Dates

Start : _____

Finished : _____

How I Got This Book

☐ Bought It

☐ Checked Out From Library

☐ Borrowed From
....

☐ Gift From
....

Favorite Quotes From The Book

Book Number

Ratings

Plot : ☆ ☆ ☆ ☆ ☆

Characters : ☐ ☐ ☐ ☐ ☐

Ease of reading : ◇ ◇ ◇ ◇ ◇

Over All : ☹ 😐 🙂

○ Paperback

○ Hardbook

○ E - Book

○ Audiobook

TITLE :

Author :

Publisher : _____   Pub. Date _____   Page Count _____

○ Fiction   ○ Non - Fiction

Genre · _____   Subject : _____

Review : _____

Dates

Start :

Finished :

How I Got This Book

☐ Bought It

☐ Checked Out From Library

☐ Borrowed From

....

☐ Gift From

....

Favorite Quotes From The Book

Ratings

Book Number

Plot : ☆ ☆ ☆ ☆ ☆

Characters : ☐ ☐ ☐ ☐ ☐

Ease of reading : ◇ ◇ ◇ ◇ ◇

Over All : ☹ 😐 ☺

○ Paperback

○ Hardbook

○ E - Book

○ Audiobook

TITLE :

Anthor :

Publisher :   Pub. Date   Page Count

○ Fiction   ○ Non - Fiction

Genre ·   Subject :

Review :

Dates

Start :

Finished :

How I Got This Book

☐ Bought It

☐ Checked Out From Library

☐ Borrowed From

....

☐ Gift From

....

Favorite Quotes From The Book

Ratings

Plot : ☆ ☆ ☆ ☆ ☆

Characters : ☐ ☐ ☐ ☐ ☐

Ease of reading : ◇ ◇ ◇ ◇ ◇

Over All : ☹ 😐 ☺

○ Paperback

○ Hardbook

○ E - Book

○ Audiobook

Rank Number

TITLE :

Anthor :

Publisher : _____ Pub. Date _____ Page Count

○ Fiction   ○ Non - Fiction

Genre : _____ Subject : _____

Review : _____

Dates

Start :

Finished :

How I Got This Book

☐ Bought It

☐ Checked Out From Library

☐ Borrowed From

....

☐ Gift From

....

Favorite Quotes From The Book

Ratings

Plot : ☆ ☆ ☆ ☆ ☆

Characters : ☐ ☐ ☐ ☐ ☐

Ease of reading : ◇ ◇ ◇ ◇ ◇

Over All : ☹ 😐 ☺

○ Paperback

○ Hardbook

○ E - Book

○ Audiobook

Book Number

TITLE :

Author :

Publisher : _____ Pub. Date _____ Page Count _____

○ Fiction   ○ Non - Fiction

Genre · _____   Subject : _____

Review : _____

Dates

Start :

Finished :

How I Got This Book

☐ Bought It

☐ Checked Out From Library

☐ Borrowed From

....

☐ Gift From

....

Favorite Quotes From The Book

Ratings

Plot : ☆ ☆ ☆ ☆ ☆

Characters : ☐ ☐ ☐ ☐ ☐

Ease of reading : ◇ ◇ ◇ ◇ ◇

Over All : ☹ 😐 🙂

Book Number

○ Paperback

○ Hardbook

○ E - Book

○ Audiobook

TITLE :

Author :

Publisher : _____ Pub. Date _____ Page Count _____

○ Fiction   ○ Non - Fiction

Genre : _____ Subject : _____

Review : _____

Dates

Start :

Finished :

How I Got This Book

☐ Bought It

☐ Checked Out From Library

☐ Borrowed From

....

☐ Gift From

....

Favorite Quotes From The Book

Ratings

Plot : ☆ ☆ ☆ ☆ ☆

Characters : ☐ ☐ ☐ ☐ ☐

Ease of reading : ◇ ◇ ◇ ◇ ◇

Over All : ☹ 😐 ☺

○ Paperback

○ Hardbook

○ E - Book

○ Audiobook

TITLE : _____

Author : _____

Publisher : _____ Pub. Date _____ Page Count _____

○ Fiction   ○ Non - Fiction

Genre : _____ Subject : _____

Review : _____
_____
_____
_____
_____
_____
_____

Dates

Start : _____

Finished : _____

How I Got This Book

☐ Bought It

☐ Checked Out From Library

☐ Borrowed From
....

☐ Gift From
....

Favorite Quotes From The Book

Ratings

Plot : ☆ ☆ ☆ ☆ ☆

Characters : ☐ ☐ ☐ ☐ ☐

Ease of reading : ◇ ◇ ◇ ◇ ◇

Over All : ☹ 😐 ☺

○ Paperback

○ Hardbook

○ E - Book

○ Audiobook

TITLE : _____

Author : _____

Publisher : _____ Pub. Date _____ Page Count _____

○ Fiction   ○ Non - Fiction

Genre · _____   Subject : _____

Review : _____
_____
_____
_____
_____
_____
_____
_____

Dates

Start :

Finished :

How I Got This Book

☐ Bought It

☐ Checked Out From Library

☐ Borrowed From

....

☐ Gift From

....

Favorite Quotes From The Book

Ratings

Book Number

Plot : ☆ ☆ ☆ ☆ ☆

Characters : ▢ ▢ ▢ ▢ ▢

Ease of reading : ◇ ◇ ◇ ◇ ◇

Over All : ☹ 😐 🙂

○ Paperback

○ Hardbook

○ E - Book

○ Audiobook

TITLE :

Anthor :

Publisher : _____ Pub. Date _____ Page Count _____

○ Fiction   ○ Non - Fiction

Genre · _____   Subject : _____

Review : _____

Dates

Start :

Finished :

How I Got This Book

☐ Bought It

☐ Checked Out From Library

☐ Borrowed From

....

☐ Gift From

....

Favorite Qyotes From The Book

Book Number

Ratings

Plot : ☆ ☆ ☆ ☆ ☆

Characters : ▢ ▢ ▢ ▢ ▢

Ease of reading : ◇ ◇ ◇ ◇ ◇

Over All : ☹ 😐 🙂

○ Paperback

○ Hardbook

○ E - Book

○ Audiobook

TITLE : _____

Anthor : _____

Publisher : _____ Pub. Date _____ Page Count _____

○ Fiction   ○ Non - Fiction

Genre · _____   Subject : _____

Review : _____

_____

_____

_____

_____

_____

_____

_____

Dates

Start : _____

Finished : _____

How I Got This Book

☐ Bought It

☐ Checked Out From Library

☐ Borrowed From

....

☐ Gift From

....

Favorite Quotes From The Book

Book Number

Ratings

Plot : ☆ ☆ ☆ ☆ ☆

Characters : ☐ ☐ ☐ ☐ ☐

Ease of reading : ◇ ◇ ◇ ◇ ◇

Over All : ☹ 😐 ☺

○ Paperback

○ Hardbook

○ E - Book

○ Audiobook

TITLE :

Author :

Publisher :   Pub. Date   Page Count

○ Fiction   ○ Non - Fiction

Genre ·   Subject :

Review :

Dates

Start :

Finished :

How I Got This Book

☐ Bought It

☐ Checked Out From Library

☐ Borrowed From

....

☐ Gift From

....

Favorite Quotes From The Book

Book Number

Ratings

Plot : ☆ ☆ ☆ ☆ ☆

Characters : ☐ ☐ ☐ ☐ ☐

Ease of reading : ◇ ◇ ◇ ◇ ◇

Over All : ☹ 😐 😊

○ Paperback

○ Hardbook

○ E - Book

○ Audiobook

TITLE :

Author :

Publisher : _____ Pub. Date _____ Page Count _____

○ Fiction   ○ Non - Fiction

Genre : _____   Subject : _____

Review : _____

_____

_____

_____

_____

_____

_____

_____

_____

Dates

Start :

Finished :

How I Got This Book

☐ Bought It

☐ Checked Out From Library

☐ Borrowed From

....

☐ Gift From

....

Favorite Quotes From The Book

Ratings

Plot : ☆ ☆ ☆ ☆ ☆

Characters : ☐ ☐ ☐ ☐ ☐

Ease of reading : ◇ ◇ ◇ ◇ ◇

Over All : ☹ 😐 😊

○ Paperback

○ Hardbook

○ E - Book

○ Audiobook

Book Number

TITLE :

Anthor :

Publisher : _____ Pub. Date _____ Page Count _____

○ Fiction   ○ Non - Fiction

Genre · _____ Subject : _____

Review : _____

Dates

Start :

Finished :

How I Got This Book

☐ Bought It

☐ Checked Out From Library

☐ Borrowed From

....

☐ Gift From

....

Favorite Quotes From The Book

Ratings

Book Number

Plot : ☆ ☆ ☆ ☆ ☆

Characters : ☐ ☐ ☐ ☐ ☐

Ease of reading : ◇ ◇ ◇ ◇ ◇

Over All : ☹ 😐 ☺

○ Paperback

○ Hardbook

○ E - Book

○ Audiobook

TITLE :

Author :

Publisher : _____ Pub. Date _____ Page Count _____

○ Fiction   ○ Non - Fiction

Genre · _____   Subject : _____

Review : _____

Dates

Start :

Finished :

How I Got This Book

☐ Bought It

☐ Checked Out From Library

☐ Borrowed From

....

☐ Gift From

....

Favorite Quotes From The Book

Book Number

Ratings

Plot : ☆ ☆ ☆ ☆ ☆

Characters : ☐ ☐ ☐ ☐ ☐

Ease of reading : ◇ ◇ ◇ ◇ ◇

Over All : ☹ 😐 🙂

○ Paperback
○ Hardbook
○ E - Book
○ Audiobook

TITLE :

Author :

Publisher : _____ Pub. Date _____ Page Count _____

○ Fiction   ○ Non - Fiction

Genre · _____   Subject : _____

Review : _____
_____
_____
_____
_____
_____
_____
_____

Dates

Start :

Finished :

How I Got This Book

☐ Bought It

☐ Checked Out From Library

☐ Borrowed From
....

☐ Gift From
....

Favorite Quotes From The Book

Book Number

Ratings

Plot : ☆ ☆ ☆ ☆ ☆

Characters : ▢ ▢ ▢ ▢ ▢

Ease of reading : ◇ ◇ ◇ ◇ ◇

Over All : ☹ 😐 ☺

○ Paperback

○ Hardbook

○ E - Book

○ Audiobook

TITLE :

Author :

Publisher : _____ Pub. Date _____ Page Count _____

○ Fiction ○ Non - Fiction

Genre : _____ Subject : _____

Review : _____

Dates

Start :

Finished :

How I Got This Book

▢ Bought It

▢ Checked Out From Library

▢ Borrowed From
....

▢ Gift From
....

Favorite Quotes From The Book

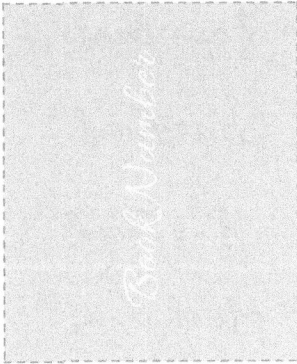

Ratings

Book Number

Plot : ☆ ☆ ☆ ☆ ☆

Characters : ☐ ☐ ☐ ☐ ☐

Ease of reading : ◇ ◇ ◇ ◇ ◇

Over All : ☹ 😐 ☺

○ Paperback

○ Hardbook

○ E - Book

○ Audiobook

TITLE :

Anthor :

Publisher : _____ Pub. Date _____ Page Count _____

○ Fiction   ○ Non - Fiction

Genre · _____ Subject : _____

Review : _____

Dates

Start :

Finished :

How I Got This Book

☐ Bought It

☐ Checked Out From Library

☐ Borrowed From
....

☐ Gift From
....

Favorite Qyotes From The Book

Book Number

Ratings

Plot : ☆ ☆ ☆ ☆ ☆

Characters : ☐ ☐ ☐ ☐ ☐

Ease of reading : ◇ ◇ ◇ ◇ ◇

Over All : ☹ 😐 🙂

○ Paperback

○ Hardbook

○ E - Book

○ Audiobook

TITLE : _____

Anthor : _____

Publisher : _____ Pub. Date _____ Page Count _____

○ Fiction   ○ Non - Fiction

Genre · _____ Subject : _____

Review : _____
_____
_____
_____
_____
_____
_____
_____
_____

Dates

Start : _____

Finished : _____

How I Got This Book

☐ Bought It

☐ Checked Out From Library

☐ Borrowed From

....

☐ Gift From

....

Favorite Quotes From The Book

Ratings

Book Number

Plot : ☆ ☆ ☆ ☆ ☆

Characters : ☐ ☐ ☐ ☐ ☐

Ease of reading : ◇ ◇ ◇ ◇ ◇

Over All : ☹ 😐 ☺

○ Paperback

○ Hardbook

○ E - Book

○ Audiobook

TITLE :

Anthor :

Publisher : _____ Pub. Date _____ Page Count _____

○ Fiction   ○ Non - Fiction

Genre · _____   Subject : _____

Review : _____

Dates

Start :

Finished :

How I Got This Book

☐ Bought It

☐ Checked Out From Library

☐ Borrowed From
....

☐ Gift From
....

Favorite Quotes From The Book

Book Number

Ratings

Plot : ☆ ☆ ☆ ☆ ☆

Characters : ☐ ☐ ☐ ☐ ☐

Ease of reading : ◇ ◇ ◇ ◇ ◇

Over All : ☹ 😐 ☺

○ Paperback

○ Hardbook

○ E - Book

○ Audiobook

TITLE :

Anthor :

Publisher : _____ Pub. Date _____ Page Count _____

○ Fiction   ○ Non - Fiction

Genre : _____   Subject : _____

Review :

Dates

Start :

Finished :

How I Got This Book

☐ Bought It

☐ Checked Out From Library

☐ Borrowed From

....

☐ Gift From

....

Favorite Quotes From The Book

Ratings

Plot : ☆ ☆ ☆ ☆ ☆

Characters : ☐ ☐ ☐ ☐ ☐

Ease of reading : ◇ ◇ ◇ ◇ ◇

Over All : ☹ 😐 🙂

○ Paperback

○ Hardbook

○ E - Book

○ Audiobook

TITLE :

Author :

Publisher : _____ Pub. Date _____ Page Count _____

○ Fiction   ○ Non - Fiction

Genre · _____   Subject : _____

Review : _____

Dates

Start :

Finished :

How I Got This Book

☐ Bought It

☐ Checked Out From Library

☐ Borrowed From

....

☐ Gift From

....

Favorite Quotes From The Book

Book Number

Ratings

Plot : ☆ ☆ ☆ ☆ ☆

Characters : ☐ ☐ ☐ ☐ ☐

Ease of reading : ◇ ◇ ◇ ◇ ◇

Over All : ☹ 😐 ☺

○ Paperback

○ Hardbook

○ E - Book

○ Audiobook

TITLE :

Anthor :

Publisher : _____ Pub. Date _____ Page Count _____

○ Fiction   ○ Non - Fiction

Genre : _____   Subject : _____

Review : _____

Dates

Start :

Finished :

How I Got This Book

☐ Bought It

☐ Checked Out From Library

☐ Borrowed From

....

☐ Gift From

....

Favorite Quotes From The Book

Book Number

Ratings

Plot : ☆ ☆ ☆ ☆ ☆

Characters : ☐ ☐ ☐ ☐ ☐

Ease of reading : ◇ ◇ ◇ ◇ ◇

Over All : ☹ 😐 ☺

○ Paperback

○ Hardbook

○ E - Book

○ Audiobook

TITLE :

Author :

Publisher :

Pub. Date

Page Count

○ Fiction

○ Non - Fiction

Genre ·

Subject :

Review :

Dates

Start :

Finished :

How I Got This Book

☐ Bought It

☐ Checked Out From Library

☐ Borrowed From

....

☐ Gift From

....

Favorite Quotes From The Book

Ratings

Plot : ☆ ☆ ☆ ☆ ☆

Characters : ☐ ☐ ☐ ☐ ☐

Ease of reading : ◇ ◇ ◇ ◇ ◇

Over All : 🙁 😐 🙂

Book Number

○ Paperback

○ Hardbook

○ E - Book

○ Audiobook

TITLE :

Author :

Publisher : _____ Pub. Date _____ Page Count _____

○ Fiction   ○ Non - Fiction

Genre · _____   Subject : _____

Review : _____

Dates

Start :

Finished :

How I Got This Book

☐ Bought It

☐ Checked Out From Library

☐ Borrowed From

....

☐ Gift From

....

Favorite Quotes From The Book

Ratings

Plot : ☆ ☆ ☆ ☆ ☆

Characters : ▢ ▢ ▢ ▢ ▢

Ease of reading : ◇ ◇ ◇ ◇ ◇

Over All : ☹ 😐 🙂

○ Paperback

○ Hardbook

○ E - Book

○ Audiobook

TITLE :

Anthor :

Publisher : _____ Pub. Date _____ Page Count _____

○ Fiction   ○ Non - Fiction

Genre : _____   Subject : _____

Review : _____

Dates

Start :

Finished :

How I Got This Book

☐ Bought It

☐ Checked Out From Library

☐ Borrowed From
....

☐ Gift From
....

Favorite Quotes From The Book

Book Number

Ratings

Plot : ☆ ☆ ☆ ☆ ☆

Characters : ☐ ☐ ☐ ☐ ☐

Ease of reading : ◇ ◇ ◇ ◇ ◇

Over All : ☹ 😐 🙂

○ Paperback

○ Hardbook

○ E - Book

○ Audiobook

TITLE : _____

Anthor : _____

Publisher : _____ Pub. Date _____ Page Count _____

○ Fiction   ○ Non - Fiction

Genre : _____   Subject : _____

Review : _____
_____
_____
_____
_____
_____
_____

Dates

Start : _____

Finished : _____

How I Got This Book

☐ Bought It

☐ Checked Out From Library

☐ Borrowed From
....

☐ Gift From
....

Favorite Quotes From The Book

Book Number

Ratings

Plot : ☆ ☆ ☆ ☆ ☆

Characters : ☐ ☐ ☐ ☐ ☐

Ease of reading : ◇ ◇ ◇ ◇ ◇

Over All : ☹ 😐 🙂

○ Paperback

○ Hardbook

○ E - Book

○ Audiobook

TITLE : _____

Anthor : _____

Publisher : _____ Pub. Date _____ Page Count _____

○ Fiction   ○ Non - Fiction

Genre · _____ Subject : _____

Review : _____

_____

_____

_____

_____

_____

_____

Dates

Start : _____

Finished : _____

How I Got This Book

☐ Bought It

☐ Checked Out From Library

☐ Borrowed From

....

☐ Gift From

....

Favorite Quotes From The Book

Ratings

Plot : ☆ ☆ ☆ ☆ ☆

Characters : ☐ ☐ ☐ ☐ ☐

Ease of reading : ◇ ◇ ◇ ◇ ◇

Over All : ☹ 😐 ☺

○ Paperback

○ Hardbook

○ E - Book

○ Audiobook

TITLE :

Anthor :

Publisher : ⎯⎯⎯⎯⎯ Pub. Date ⎯⎯⎯⎯⎯ Page Count ⎯⎯⎯⎯

○ Fiction   ○ Non - Fiction

Genre · ⎯⎯⎯⎯⎯ Subject : ⎯⎯⎯⎯⎯

Review :

Dates

Start :

Finished :

How I Got This Book

☐ Bought It

☐ Checked Out From Library

☐ Borrowed From
⎯⎯⎯⎯⎯⎯⎯⎯⎯

☐ Gift From
⎯⎯⎯⎯⎯⎯⎯⎯⎯

Favorite Quotes From The Book

Ratings

Plot : ☆ ☆ ☆ ☆ ☆

Characters : ☐ ☐ ☐ ☐ ☐

Ease of reading : ◇ ◇ ◇ ◇ ◇

Over All : 🙁 😐 🙂

○ Paperback

○ Hardbook

○ E - Book

○ Audiobook

Book Number

TITLE :

Anthor :

Publisher : _____ Pub. Date _____ Page Count _____

○ Fiction   ○ Non - Fiction

Genre : _____   Subject : _____

Review :

Dates

Start :

Finished :

How I Got This Book

☐ Bought It

☐ Checked Out From Library

☐ Borrowed From
....

☐ Gift From
....

Favorite Qyotes From The Book

Book Number

Ratings

Plot : ☆ ☆ ☆ ☆ ☆

Characters : ▢ ▢ ▢ ▢ ▢

Ease of reading : ◇ ◇ ◇ ◇ ◇

Over All : ☹ 😐 🙂

○ Paperback

○ Hardbook

○ E - Book

○ Audiobook

TITLE :

Anthor :

Publisher : .... Pub. Date .... Page Count ....

○ Fiction   ○ Non - Fiction

Genre · ....   Subject : ....

Review : ....

Dates

Start :

Finished :

How I Got This Book

☐ Bought It

☐ Checked Out From Library

☐ Borrowed From

....

☐ Gift From

....

Favorite Quotes From The Book

Book Number

Ratings

Plot : ☆ ☆ ☆ ☆ ☆

Characters : ☐ ☐ ☐ ☐ ☐

Ease of reading : ◇ ◇ ◇ ◇ ◇

Over All : ☹ 😐 🙂

○ Paperback

○ Hardbook

○ E - Book

○ Audiobook

TITLE :

Anthor :

Publisher : _____ Pub. Date _____ Page Count _____

○ Fiction   ○ Non - Fiction

Genre · _____   Subject : _____

Review : _____

Dates

Start :

Finished :

How I Got This Book

☐ Bought It

☐ Checked Out From Library

☐ Borrowed From

....

☐ Gift From

....

Favorite Quotes From The Book

Book Number

Ratings

Plot : ☆ ☆ ☆ ☆ ☆

Characters : ☐ ☐ ☐ ☐ ☐

Ease of reading : ◇ ◇ ◇ ◇ ◇

Over All : ☹ 😐 ☺

○ Paperback

○ Hardbook

○ E - Book

○ Audiobook

TITLE :

Author :

Publisher : _____ Pub. Date _____ Page Count _____

○ Fiction   ○ Non - Fiction

Genre · _____   Subject : _____

Review : _____

Dates

Start :

Finished :

How I Got This Book

☐ Bought It

☐ Checked Out From Library

☐ Borrowed From

....

☐ Gift From

....

Favorite Quotes From The Book

Book Number

Ratings

Plot : ☆ ☆ ☆ ☆ ☆

Characters : ☐ ☐ ☐ ☐ ☐

Ease of reading : ◇ ◇ ◇ ◇ ◇

Over All : ☹ ☺ ☺

○ Paperback

○ Hardbook

○ E - Book

○ Audiobook

TITLE :

Author :

Publisher : _____ Pub. Date _____ Page Count _____

○ Fiction   ○ Non - Fiction

Genre · _____ Subject : _____

Review : _____

Dates

Start :

Finished :

How I Got This Book

☐ Bought It

☐ Checked Out From Library

☐ Borrowed From

....

☐ Gift From

....

Favorite Quotes From The Book

Book Number

Ratings

Plot : ☆ ☆ ☆ ☆ ☆

Characters : ☐ ☐ ☐ ☐ ☐

Ease of reading : ◇ ◇ ◇ ◇ ◇

Over All : ☹ 😐 🙂

○ Paperback

○ Hardbook

○ E - Book

○ Audiobook

TITLE :

Author :

Publisher : _____ Pub. Date _____ Page Count _____

○ Fiction   ○ Non - Fiction

Genre : _____   Subject : _____

Review : _____

Dates

Start :

Finished :

How I Got This Book

☐ Bought It

☐ Checked Out From Library

☐ Borrowed From

....

☐ Gift From

....

Favorite Quotes From The Book

Book Number

Ratings

Plot : ☆ ☆ ☆ ☆ ☆

Characters : ☐ ☐ ☐ ☐ ☐

Ease of reading : ◇ ◇ ◇ ◇ ◇

Over All : ⌢ ⊡ ☺

○ Paperback

○ Hardbook

○ E - Book

○ Audiobook

TITLE :

Anthor :

Publisher : _____ Pub. Date _____ Page Count _____

○ Fiction   ○ Non - Fiction

Genre · _____   Subject : _____

Review : _____

Dates

Start :

Finished :

How I Got This Book

☐ Bought It

☐ Checked Out From Library

☐ Borrowed From

....

☐ Gift From

....

Favorite Quotes From The Book

Book Number

Ratings

Plot : ☆ ☆ ☆ ☆ ☆

Characters : ☐ ☐ ☐ ☐ ☐

Ease of reading : ◇ ◇ ◇ ◇ ◇

Over All : ☹ 😐 🙂

○ Paperback

○ Hardbook

○ E - Book

○ Audiobook

TITLE :

Anthor :

Publisher : _____   Pub. Date _____   Page Count _____

○ Fiction   ○ Non - Fiction

Genre · _____   Subject : _____

Review : _____

Dates

Start :

Finished :

How I Got This Book

☐ Bought It

☐ Checked Out From Library

☐ Borrowed From

....

☐ Gift From

....

Favorite Quotes From The Book

Ratings

Plot : ☆ ☆ ☆ ☆ ☆

Characters : ☐ ☐ ☐ ☐ ☐

Ease of reading : ◇ ◇ ◇ ◇ ◇

Over All : ☹ 😐 ☺

○ Paperback
○ Hardbook
○ E - Book
○ Audiobook

Book Number

TITLE :

Author :

Publisher : _____ Pub. Date _____ Page Count _____

○ Fiction   ○ Non - Fiction

Genre : _____   Subject : _____

Review : _____

Dates

Start :

Finished :

How I Got This Book

☐ Bought It

☐ Checked Out From Library

☐ Borrowed From
....

☐ Gift From
....

Favorite Quotes From The Book

Ratings

Book Number

Plot : ☆ ☆ ☆ ☆ ☆

Characters : ☐ ☐ ☐ ☐ ☐

Ease of reading : ◇ ◇ ◇ ◇ ◇

Over All : ☹ ☺ ☺

○ Paperback

○ Hardbook

○ E - Book

○ Audiobook

TITLE :

Anthor :

Publisher :   Pub. Date   Page Count

○ Fiction   ○ Non - Fiction

Genre :   Subject :

Review :

Dates

Start :

Finished :

How I Got This Book

☐ Bought It

☐ Checked Out From Library

☐ Borrowed From

☐ Gift From

Favorite Quotes From The Book

Book Number

Ratings

Plot : ☆ ☆ ☆ ☆ ☆

Characters : ☐ ☐ ☐ ☐ ☐

Ease of reading : ◇ ◇ ◇ ◇ ◇

Over All : ☹ 😐 ☺

○ Paperback

○ Hardbook

○ E - Book

○ Audiobook

TITLE :

Anthor :

Publisher :

Pub. Date

Page Count

○ Fiction   ○ Non - Fiction

Genre ·

Subject :

Review :

Dates

Start :

Finished :

How I Got This Book

☐ Bought It

☐ Checked Out From Library

☐ Borrowed From

....

☐ Gift From

....

Favorite Quotes From The Book